Zen Pig

Volume 1 / Issue 1

written by:
mark brown

illustrated by:
amy lynn larwig

each copy sold gives
1 person clean water
for 1 year

Come say "Hi!" to Zen Pig online:
ZenPigBook.com

Don't forget, Zen Pig loves seeing pictures of his new home and new friends -
#ZenPig on Instagram to send them his way!

Dedicated to my son Noble, who is already a far better man than I.

I love you.

Eons ago
On a green grassy knoll,
Lived a pleasant little pig
Who always seemed quite whole.

He enjoyed his life
Much more than most
Because he took the time
To look at things close.

Where ever he was,
He was always there,
Ready and willing
To be fully aware.

"That Zen Pig is special."
Is what others would say.
Yet, Zen Pig denied, and said,
"I'll show you the way.

Care for each other,
As much as yourself.
And never lose sight,
That love is true wealth.

And when you speak
Choose your words with care.
Only kindness and compassion
Will ease others' despair.

We all make mistakes,
So forgive yourself fast.
Don't expect to be perfect
Or happiness won't last.

Never waste time
Thinking of the future or the past.
Just enjoy this moment
And all that it has.

Be thankful for all that you have,
There is no need for more.
You have everything that's needed
To walk through happy's door.

When someone's in need
Don't think, just act.
Give all that you can
And don't hold back.

Listen to my words
And follow the path.
Then you too will sit atop the knoll
With the green, green grass."

Namaste.
("The light in me loves the light in you.")

_____'s Zen Pig Collection

☐ Zen Pig   ☐ The Wonder We Are   ☐ All That Is Needed

☐ Where You'll Find Love   ☐ Here to Do   ☐ To be announced...

It's hard to believe that even today, so many still do not have access to clean water.

But YOU are helping.

Digging new wells, building fences to keep livestock from contaminating sources, repairing existing wells, and constructing toilet slabs give much needed help to communities in need.

Thank You.

What is one thing YOU are grateful for?